Don't Shoot the Customer!

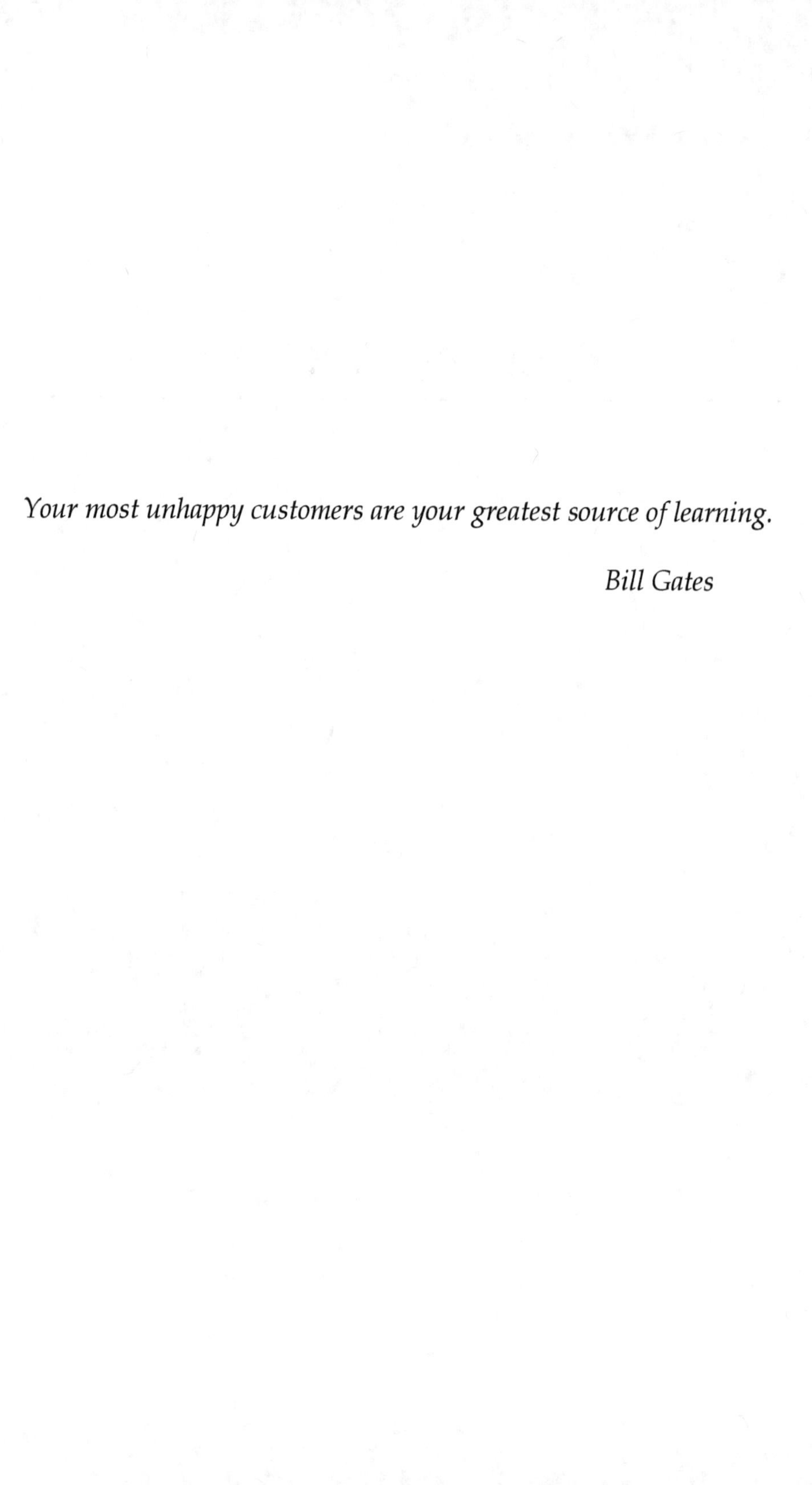

Your most unhappy customers are your greatest source of learning.

Bill Gates

Don't Shoot the Customer!

Derek Warinner

Lorraine Guerra

Illustrated by Sarah Warinner

First Printing: 2020

ISBN 978-1-67801-359-2

Guiding Thought

When you contemplate a problem, the process of solving it
has already begun.

Contents

Introduction

"You wouldn't believe what MY CUSTOMER did!"

It was a couple hours before boarding time for our flights, and for once we were early enough to meet for a beverage! Your authors were headed out to different points that day, eager to compare notes on trips past and present.

Neither of us smoked, but there was something comfortable about this place. Thin wafts of cigar smoke streaming by, a gentle hubbub. Two men in grey suits struck up a conversation, truly lamenting how they apparently had been taken for a long, painful ride on a deal they couldn't possibly make any money on!

We couldn't help but get drawn into it. We asked a couple of pointed questions which shocked the two men at first – until they saw we meant well. They offered us a cigar (politely declined, not that we'd necessarily mind) and the conversation went on. And on. They finally returned to the bar for another beverage.

Our ears perked up to a second conversation that sounded a little bit too familiar. This customer talk seemed to be catchy!

The little bar napkins were often fun to draw on. We sketched one of the scenes at the bar. Then we grabbed a second…. a third. By the time we left for our flights, we had a small collection of these sketches. With a much bigger recollection of all those situations where customers of all shapes and sizes seemingly had the upper hand, "taking us for a ride."

These are those memories.

You want WHAT?!

"Don't judge a book by its cover."

It's true.

But most people judge it anyway.

Only the highest recommendation from a friend, acclaimed reviewer or critic can overcome a crappy book cover. The cover is the beautiful Ribeye Steak showcased in a plastic sealed wrapper. The cover is the "SIZZLE," not a piece of meat. It's like a "peepshow", it tells a little, but it SHOWS a LOT! So, your author was looking for a hot shot artist to do a sizzling book cover. She thought she had a great idea!

"There's gonna be a gun on the cover and the title is 'Don't Shoot the Customer'."

She thought to herself, "where could I find an artist?"

A classical, trained professional artist wouldn't take this project – she needed someone with a little bit of EDGE for this, maybe a LOT of EDGE.

Aha! Tattoo parlor!

She walked into the best "cutting edge" tattoo shop in town. Tattoo toters walked around everywhere, displaying piercings and more that don't really need to be mentioned here.

She was, of course, dressed for success. Business suit, briefcase, perfect hair, pumps, (in a Tattoo Parlor).

"Can I help you?" Friendly, tattooed and edgy counter person asks.

Don't Shoot the Customer!

She shared the spiel. "It's 'Don't Shoot the Customer'. I need a book cover with a gun on it that conveys this message. Artwork. Oh, and it needs to be funny!"

"Huh?"

With a blank stare, the artist scratched her head.
She goes to the back and emerges with another artist, the owner of the shop. Same spiel.

The owner said, "Let me get this right; You want us to draw this on paper, and you don't want us to give you a tattoo, and you want it to be funny?"

They didn't think that was very funny.
"We don't draw."

"Whaddya mean you don't draw? How do you draw tattoos?"
The owner pointed to the door.
"Get out, lady."

Can you believe it? They had kicked me out – me, a walking blank canvas, a customer that would have paid a small fortune for the art (compared with a tattoo, at least) and maybe residuals!

And who knows... maybe a tattoo, as well?
Don't Shoot the Customer!
Thank them for the opportunity to think outside the box.

The Billboard

As the company grows, so do you.

After a few years in business, we were able to set aside funds for advertising. It was a BIG STEP! What was that next step?

Top of Mind Awareness.

You need to make your customers think about you even when they aren't with you or seeking your goods or services. How do customers see you so much they have you memorized? Trying to figure this out, the subtle answer was there, disguised as a co-worker.

"You need to advertise on a billboard."

That's silly, I'm not going to put our business on a billboard. A few weeks pass and the same co-worker brings up this billboard idea, again! I don't know why it irritated me, but it did. Then he goes on to say how he had one, and a customer of his would call him and say he shot holes in it.

I said, "Oh, for crying out loud, that sounds horrible! Why would I pay for a billboard with my business on it to be used as a shooting range? Sounds like a waste of money to me."

He laughed and said, "Don't you get it? The guy called ME and he was letting me know how he saw my advertisement." That is a funny way of telling you.

I thought about what he said, and that last phrase stuck with me. So, I thought, "I'll try it, though I'm not sure what I will put on it. I need to know that this works."

If I only put business information on it, most customers won't remember where they saw your billboard, or print advertising, or where they heard about the business when you ask on the follow up survey. They will say whatever first pops into their head. I admit, I used to do that before I realized how essential this information is to business owners.

I came up with a bright idea – I will put my face, and my business partner's face, on the billboard with some words in the middle about our business. The who, what, where info. Two blondes on the billboard. We did cause a few traffic jams at first, but traffic eventually settled down. Now we needed to know if they were seeing blondes, or seeing our business ad.

I started getting calls from people I knew. "Hey, I saw you on a billboard on the highway." That shifted to strangers coming up to me in the grocery store. "Hey, aren't you the one on that billboard?" Nothing about the business, though.

I guessed it was too many blondes and not enough about the business. They were not sure what we did, but they knew we did something. We were getting plenty of attention but needed more focus on getting our business information out there.

Funny thing happened after we took the billboard down. Customers kept saying they saw us on the billboard, even after it had been down for a year! The billboard had "staying power" and developed that top of mind awareness. Our business message had been received, after all!

I don't want to hear it!

It takes months to find a customer… seconds to lose one.

Vince Lombardi

Tony's face was red with anger. What could have set him off this badly, this early in the morning?

It was 15 minutes before the customer meeting was to begin. Your author had come in early, to set up the projector and presentation slides.

The boss had called up to my office a few minutes before. "Tony's mad that you're not down here setting up."

What was the difference, I thought – I was going to carry in a laptop with slides queued, to start the meeting?

Appearances were everything in this situation. I offered this defense, or started to, at least.

Don't Shoot the Customer!

"I don't want to hear it!"

As it turned out, the meeting went without a hitch. Good thing, too. Imagine how much hot water your author would have been in, if anything went awry?

Our internal customer's reaction was a bit on the extreme side, though. But I swallowed my pride and let things ride, for the time being.

The next time this same customer showed up, they came early! An hour early. There was no way that I could see, to be ready for that! But there was a lesson to be learned here.

Customers do what they want. It's up to us to be there when they need us.

What happens in Vegas...

Imagine if losing weight was as easy as losing my keys...

Excerpt from Rotten E Card

The three musketeers were headed to Vegas to show their newest product. Porthos had inherited management of the new product from its previous champion, a well-known fencing master. He had lost several duels and, with them, the favor of the Queen.

Porthos invited Athos (who had fought at the previous champion's side) and Aramis (who usually was engaged in other conflicts) to join him at the show. He had three heavy crates packed with wares and sent to the land of glitter and gold.

The musketeers arrived and made haste to the convention center. Their crates had been brought to their proper location. In a couple of hours, they would be ready to wow and dazzle showgoers with their product.

"Did you bring your key, Porthos?"

Athos was all too familiar with these crates. They were each secured with a padlock to prevent would-be thieves from having an early sample. Locked they were – and the key Porthos had not.

Matters would shortly go from bad to worse as Porthos slowly realized that the location setup was not completed. Additionally, one key crate with the graphic designs had not been dispatched with the other three. Porthos did not even know this crate was to be part of the shipment! He was starting to wonder how long he could curry his own favor with the Queen, with the situation deteriorating as it was.

Don't Shoot the Customer!

The musketeers began repairing things with a visit to the mercantile for needed supplies. The locks came off, orders were dispatched for immediate carriage of the fourth mystery crate, and Athos went into high gear as he began setting up the display. Aramis began poking around to find supportive locals who could help with the electrical supply and carpeting.

By morning, the display still looked shameful as the fourth crate had not arrived. The floor was in and supply run for the animated display. Customers were still coming by to see the product, and Athos did what he could to make a sales pitch without graphics. Aramis ran about procuring additional supplies to patch things up.

Though many customers passed by without the completed display, eventually all came together, and the show's 2nd and 3rd day were quite effective. Did anything else happen? Well, they were in Vegas…

Lessons learned – always have a local contact or two who is interested in helping. And – check your sh*t before shipping it out.

We've gotta change the rope for the church bell!

The difference between stupidity and genius… is that genius has its limits.

Albert Einstein

Our venue was originally an old church, with a traditional church bell. The bell has a wonderful sound that echoes throughout the town, marking the beginning of special events.

The guy who originally set up the bell rope was a knot artist, or maybe someone with a twisted sense of humor. He tied it with a 10-loop noose, like you'd see on the old Western shows.

We were planning to change that to something more civilized looking. We waited one couple too long.

We hosted a beautiful wedding and reception for a lovely couple, their family and friends. We thought everything had gone wonderfully (as it usually does). We were wrong.

Later, we discovered the groom used a bit of his private time to call his friends around our bell rope. "Hey, take my picture in this!" He put his head in the noose. Can you imagine?

We were more than imagining. We were experiencing the knowledge of that moment in living color. And our staff started with the jokes, "They HUNG around too long," and "Our customers are gonna HANG us out to dry!" One of the bartenders said, "How did we get ROPED into this job!"

DON'T SHOOT THE CUSTOMER!

As the photo started to hit the Internet, we frantically started untying the knot artist's work! We were glad that no one got hurt – including the bride!

We didn't shoot the customer, either (though perhaps he deserved it, if only a little, maybe some ROPE BURN)!

We retied the knots, immediately, into a much more pleasant design with lush tassels on the end, more fitting for a wedding ceremony!

Then we all looked around our venue for other "little details" to clean up before the next wedding; we didn't want to stick our NECK out again!

A chilly situation

Swallowing your pride occasionally will never give you indigestion.

Unknown

A potato processing line is a modern marvel... raw potatoes go in one end, and frozen French fries come out from the other, ready to bake or fry. Tons of stainless sheet metal, fluid vats, cutters, sprayers, food safe motors, belts, and PLC's manage the stuff in between which peels the potatoes, cuts them into long squarish slices, washes, par-fries, and freezes them into those ever-so-consistent French fries sold by the bag in your friendly neighborhood grocer's freezer section.

A company that we worked with had installed a new commercial freezer at one of these potato processing plants.

The freezer module is a stacked belt forced air (some would say "blast") freezer that spreads out the fries for rapid freezing. The freezer delivers to the job site in pieces, and a 4-man crew takes 7-10 days to assemble the belt and drive system, along with welding together the stainless enclosure. Like many other projects completed before, we sent our field tech and crew out to the plant, laid out the install, shipped in the gear, welded hundreds of feet of stainless steel seams, aligned the mechanism, welded and bolted it in place, mounted the belt and controller, and started up the freezer.

As our tech and the crew returned home, we thought the project was headed into the year's success reel. We were already thinking about reviewing the completed project's financials.

But we were about to have a real "blast", as it were!

We received an email from the customer with pictures of metal fragments which had shown up in the fries, tripping the metal detector. One

Don't Shoot the Customer!

or two frags were bad enough, but then it grew to 7…. Then 10…. And we had to send out our best tech to the site to have a look around.

There were a lot of potential sources of metal on a fry line, but we needed to be sure the fragments were not coming from the freezer.

Sure enough, the crew didn't do a good job of cleaning up. Our tech began the meticulous process of cleaning the freezer and trying to cool off the customer who understandably was quite upset.

After a week of cleaning, we sent two managers over to run a follow up inspection and find a way to bring closure to the thing. Saturday was a full day for all of us as we reviewed the findings and made our way through the freezer installation, looking for any remaining fragments.

We showed up onsite Sunday morning to continue. At this point the site manager made it a point to say that he and his crew never worked on Sunday, to make sure that they all could attend church with their families and rest. After this conversation, he promptly left (for church, we assume) and wasn't seen again until Monday.

Apparently, the Sunday "sabbath" didn't apply to suppliers, especially those who botched an installation on the potato line!

It was understandable, right? We were in the wrong. We were there to fix it. We were fixing it. If we needed to work Sunday, then that's what we needed.

Something in the gut didn't sit right with the situation. Religion should transcend worldly affairs! We're not saying that the site manager should have invited us to church (though that would have been a fine idea – for all he knew, we were heathens who also needed to do some heavenly business). A comment to say that he would understand if we took Sunday morning off, would have gone a long way.

We had our "Sunday Service" right there on the line, complete with the smell of production chemicals, motors, stainless steel, and the clean-in-place chemicals, a signature aroma of many food processing facilities.

Continuing to inspect – seek, and we shall find. Removing every particle, even if not in the production path. Doing the job that should have been done before.

That customer stayed fussy for several weeks after we left. He made triply sure that we understood how badly we upset his potato cart! But don't shoot the customer.

This was a lesson on how to "do it right" the first time! And with that, a free "live training" on navigating our way through a bad situation. We took the opportunity to swallow our pride, admit fault, and figure out how to (1) prevent this from happening in the future, and (2) speed up our response if it ever did.

Would you like fries with that?

Don't mess with Texas

"I'm writing this email to let you know
that I am TAKING MY BUSINESS ELSEWHERE,
but since nobody has gotten back to me on my LAST
THREE EMAILS, you probably won't see this note
ANYWAY, and WON'T EVEN KNOW!"

This customer was a little bit on the needy side. He was a pseudo-regular buyer of our steel products, who could spend a pretty good penny with us when he wanted to. I must admit, this wasn't the first time he sent a threatening email. It was the first time he said he was pulling his business, though.

What had happened?

His orders were probably a few days late. 10 working days tops. Yes, that's bad, even though not unheard of in his industry. No, it shouldn't be enough to cause him to walk away from us!

If he really sent 3 emails and we didn't respond, though, that would be bad. We sent an apology and had our local agent stop by to try and smooth things over. Reportedly, he had calmed down by the time of the visit and all was now well.

We saw him at a conference a month or two later – he greeted us as if nothing had happened!

Don't shoot the customer, though. Especially in Texas – the customer might shoot back!

We try just as hard these days to get his business – but we must admit, when he flies off the handle on the email, it's more difficult to take him seriously. All the same, we made sure the sales desk was trained to make sure he got a response and "felt the love" when he needed something!

Our first rodeo

The customer's perception is your reality.

Kate Zabriskie

"Good morning!" Our first customer (yes, our first one EVER) came through the church doors, ready to start her wedding day. She had our Introductory coupon for $250 discounted off a wedding package that normally cost $300, for hosting at our venue.

"Nice to see you! Let's get started!" It was 7AM, and the wedding wasn't going to be until 3PM. Don't get me wrong, this was truly a momentous occasion! The culmination of months of planning, effort, wrangling, toil and tears. We made the vision boards, acquired the property (a deconsecrated church in rough shape, but in an incredible location) and completely renovated the venue. We went to the banker, the city clerk, the Permit Department, the insurance company, and several contractors. We brought our tools, our relatives, our friends, we hired, fired, gardened, trained ourselves and our staff and got the job done. It was finally D-Day and time to start this business with a BANG! Now for the big reveal, showcasing the newest and greatest wedding and events venue in our small town.

The venue was tip-top; flowers were on every table, lace dollies were under every antique lamp, 4-inch white ribbon bows adorned each row of chairs. Decorated gift bags were ready at the bar with a sweet offer to bring in those first customers. Response to the big reveal was great, except our small-town scene had dog races on the event calendar that weekend. So what, dog races couldn't compare to the GRAND OPENING of the most beautiful wedding venue in the Midwest! We greeted and entertained so many visitors, and their 4-legged friends, that we began to think the dog races were going to begin at our front gate! As the reveal went on, we were on the edge of our proverbial seats. How many visitors were going to bite on our HUGE DISCOUNT OFFER? Most, if not all, of the gift bags were still sitting there, and it wasn't until near the end of the reveal that our first real prospect walked up. "I'd like to have my wedding here!" We smiled graciously, but on the inside, it was pure pandemonium in our hearts! YIPPEE or OH NO! Our first customer!

The bride to be was holding the coupon from the gift bag and wanted to discuss her wedding to be held only one week away. We were offering a limited time coupon to a few brides and grooms in the right place, at the right time, to have a grand wedding. The coupon was worth $250 towards a $300 full-service ceremony. We anticipated most couples would book the wedding and a reception with us so with the full-service reception cost of $1,800, we could come out all right. This is real, we're booking our first wedding!

Then came the punch line. "I'll be here at 7AM next Saturday to get my hair and makeup done and dress. The wedding will be at 3PM, and we'll have all the photos taken, but we must be out of here before 6PM. Our reception hall is going to kick us out at midnight, and we don't want to start late."

We kept on rolling that smile. Roll that smile. Did she just book us for the whole day? For a short wedding service? As if to add insult to injury, she asked if the booking came with complimentary drinks! I mentioned that, especially at a venue like this one, the couple would often book both the wedding AND the reception. We would be $1,850 on the positive side, for what would be a long day and night. This bride had no intention of that. Her reception had been booked months ago and they were going to be married in their own church. When we opened up, offering that coupon, she realized she could be married in the most beautiful venue in the area, for $50, about what she would pay the officiant at her church! Marry and run was her game. Run, that is, from her $50 beautiful, fabulous wedding venue to her $12,000 reception hall.

Just before sunrise, at zero dark thirty that spring morning, our assembled staff exchanged glances trying to hide our anger at the bride to be, who we knew, was obviously taking advantage of us. Our sweet first customer came through the venue doors, heading to the bridal suite with

Don't Shoot the Customer!

her coupon in hand (almost as if it was a Magic Wand), ready to get pampered for her special day. Lights, camera, makeup, and POOF, a bride-to-be became a beautiful bride as the hairspray (like a beautiful aura) settled on the floor. She requested, we ran to retrieve whatever was needed, provide any assistance required. Whatever her needs were, were far outnumbered by our need for a five-star rating on this wedding!

As the very long day wore on, fatigue set in; not good when trying to maintain rationality and provide excellent Five Star service. We kept going, knowing it would finally end by 6pm, the bride's deadline to leave for her $12,000 reception.

Wait, who's in charge here? Who's holding the reins on this bucking bronco of a bride? We had, unknowingly, handed the reins to our customer.

The wedding went off without a hitch, the beautiful bride floated through our beautiful, terraced gardens, music filled the air, so sweet to your ears. We received several compliments on how beautiful and seamless the wedding turned out. Somehow, we made it look effortless. The bride thanked us for a beautiful event, with hugs and waves as they drove off to their $12,000 reception. We bandaged our "wounds", trying not to think about the earth shattering $50.00 of revenue our venue received for our efforts. Maybe it would have been easier to open a chapel in Vegas.

With tired feet and exhausted minds, we realized, DON'T SHOOT THE CUSTOMER! Thank them. She had taught us a valuable lesson. Spell out your offering, thoughtfully, carefully – consider the language you use and the importance of timing, profit/loss and the exposure your promotions will bring. Make sure to always read the fine print you've written and let a lawyer, or someone you trust, review the offers. Don't bury yourself, or the customer, in legalese and excessive terms and conditions. Ensure your committed resources don't exceed the value you're offering (and expect to be paid for).

Always make sure YOU are riding the bull, and the bull is not riding YOU!

Let's Go!

Runaway cost

"If your graph is right, I might as well turn in my resignation, right now!"

The last Cost Manager had taken a new job within the company – once the ink was dry, he left so fast you could see the smoke from his tire tracks. He was gone! We wondered what he was running away from – but didn't have to wonder for long.

The first cost analysis on the new dozer on the drawing board showed a very large cost increase from the earlier version now in production. Cost Managers were there to watch the cost of new development, highlighting where costs were going up so Engineering could try to redesign some of it back down again. The market wouldn't take kindly to a new dozer at twice the price!

Your author had built his first waterfall chart, with a big red bar. Was that part of the job? Yes. Was it supposed to be that big before somebody knew about it? No.

The commentator above was a big-shot, a Senior Vice President of Development – he, along with two other kingpins, ran the show, sometimes leading in front, and at other times behind the scenes. There was no way his trusted associates in Engineering would raise the cost that much without telling him.

"How could that be?"

Naturally, the first assumption was that the newbie was wrong. I can't say I wouldn't have said the same myself. But now comes the grisly part.

To prove him wrong, said VP started a herculean effort to "prove" that the costs were not as we said they were. My guess is that he spent at least $500K of the group's time in a highly visible, but poorly coordinated, effort. At one point the Development Director said, "we're coming up with so much data – how come nobody is using it?" Hint, genius. Probably not the right data.

After the most expensive audit of a development program in modern history (or so we thought!) the conclusion was that each product cost was within $200 (or less than 1%) of the accurate number.

Sigh of relief for yours truly. Groan of dismay for the product manager, as Engineering's new design had thoroughly torpedoed his budget. Your other author had the dubious honor of reporting budget status in the later months… a growing deficit that program leaders did not want to admit to.

Our first instinct was to run away, like that Cost Manager at the beginning of our story.

But, don't shoot the customer.

Don't Shoot the Customer!

When you can see it coming – this kind of a problem is a gold mine, for you! It might be a bit uncomfortable to manage from inside the group, trying to dodge bullets in this politically charged situation. However, if you run into this from the outside, you are the hero! Ride in on your war horse – save your customer millions.

Size matters

Sometimes the boss can be a bit of a Negative Nancy.

One that we knew, would tell an elaborate story about why the deal won't work, why the customer won't treat us right, why we can't meet their requirements. Why the competitor will stupidly offer bottom dollar to get the deal.

"But look, we can try offer 'A', like we did with customer 'B'…" his team member offers, tentatively.

"Alright, Mr. Big Nuts Ding Dong, why don't you try that!"

But you know what he is really saying. It's not going to work, and he told you so.

To make matters worse, the boss freely admits that he borrowed this expression from a former boss of his, with a bigger ego and, we assume, an even better endowment. How often would an employee reasonably tolerate this talk? Once a year? Once a week?

In this story, "Mr. Big…" was mentioned often enough that we wonder if some team members hung up their skates at times, in frustration (or mild disgust).

Don't run off to HR yet, though. Don't quit, either. First things first. Try that idea you had. Make it work, if you can. If you do… well… the boss might have to backpedal a little bit. But don't get your hopes up. Likely there's another loophole he can point to.

When you get that win – find another one. And a third. I'm guessing that, after racking up a few, you won't hear much more of that borrowed expression.

Will the real Mr. Big Nuts Ding Dong please stand up?

Not in MY theater!

Here's an old story with as much meaning now, as it did back in the day.

Broadway had defined the theater experience as high-society – attendees came dressed in their finest to enjoy the company of their peers and view the best live entertainment in the form of plays and concerts.

Movie theaters were started along the same theme, trying to appeal to the same customers with their silent pictures projected on the silver screen in finely decorated houses. As long as the paradigm held, movies were kept away from the masses with this society image.

Don't Shoot the Customer!

When movies added sound in the late 20's, they appealed to a much larger potential base of customers. Attendance swelled, with tens of millions visiting theaters weekly for a cheap diversion.

Where theaters had kept out food (especially street food) which was supported by their appeal to elegance, now large audiences wanted something to eat as they enjoyed their movie experience.

Enter popcorn – a popular street food, available for 5-10 cents a bag. Folks brought bags of popcorn into the theater (likely, against theater rules!) – and theater owners caught on. Provide the convenience of offering theater-popped popcorn to customers, against their better judgment. Make money on both ticket sales and snack sales. This formula ended up being the salvation of many theaters in the 1930's when ticket sales slumped and having two revenue streams supported profitability.

Be careful that your rules aren't keeping out customers – and watch for the rule breakers that could be bringing you your next business model!

Pass the popcorn, please…

Somebody does what Nobody did

There's no traffic on the extra mile.

Roger Staubauch
Dallas Cowboys

"Would you PLEASE stop that?"

A major vendor was miffed at your author. It was our practice to pack up our brides' decorations and personal items after each wedding. It was a no-brainer to us; sure, it was more work for our staff. And, YES, by controlling that effort we had MUCH MORE control over when the event was completed, to stay within the contracted time and go home afterward to OUR personal lives.

Hmmm. Our vendors didn't think that was proper. They preferred, we were certain, to pack up their items as soon as their parts were completed. Remember, our venue was an all-in-one location – dressing room, wedding chapel, beautiful manicured gardens, reception venue.   All the pieces needed to stay assembled until the reception ended. Many families like to go back upstairs and take their own candid photographs, using the decorations they paid for. If the florist high-tailed it out with the decorative flowers, the chapel would look bare and un-EVENT-ful. When they left, it forced our staff to button up the venue! We pay our staff well, but we also recommended and paid for the vendors' participation. Our vendors regularly complained about this. WHY, was a mystery.

We finally realized that as a TEAM we were stronger than individuals. As a team we put on a better wedding EVENT, not only a ceremony. As a TEAM we added VALUE to each other's participation; the military calls

Don't Shoot the Customer!

that a FORCE MULTIPLIER. In return for our high level of perfor-
mance, the bride, her family and friends received a greater value. All of
us benefited from working together till the end of the event.

Our CUSTOMERS loved our attention to DETAIL.

Now, all the other venues in town do the same thing.

Thanks, Vendors, for embracing our changes that led to our
EVOLUTION into an AWARD-WINNING wedding destination in our
state and nationwide.

GO TEAM!

Doing what no one else has done.

His Take-Away

I feel like I'm waiting on something that isn't going to happen.
Don't complain; just work harder.

Randy Pausch

Ocean freight can be a tricky thing.

We had shipped a brand-new aircraft tow tractor from Savannah port in Georgia, headed to the Middle East. To do that, our company had to invest a lot of up front time and money to work with freight forwarders and carriers to ensure the tractor would be prepped at the port and loaded to ships in the right way to prevent damage. We had it together… or so we thought.

Several weeks later, our customer called to say that we had missed his due date. Of course, missing a date is never a good thing. How was it

Don't Shoot the Customer!

last time you missed one? And this customer had no shortage of drama, as the world's major airports all revolved around the use of this one tractor. If the tractor wasn't commissioned on time, planes would be grounded, right?

Probably not. Most operators had fleets of tractors – being down one would overwork the others a little bit. And this customer had been down one since he ordered this new one – for the manufacturing and planned shipping time.

He made us think it was a national emergency, though. We pressured our freight forwarder to find out what happened – apparently the ship had to offload some cargo at an intermediate port. Within a couple of weeks, we were assured, the tractor would be loaded to a new vessel and be back on its way!

We let the customer know. Problem solved… or so we thought.

A week later we got a call. The customer was upset that we didn't immediately trans-load the tractor to the first pirate ship that called the port. When we didn't do that, he took it upon himself to do so.

Now, the tractor was on a local vessel. Our freight forwarder had lost control of the shipment. I guess the unit delivered fine, perhaps a week or two late instead of the 3-4 weeks that our forwarder would normally have accomplished. It could easily have been lost in transit due to the customer stepping in the middle of the shipment.

But the best part was yet to come!

The invoice fell due. Upon follow up, the customer advised that "because of our incompetence" he would not be paying for the tractor. So, he was out a couple grand for the trans-shipment, and we were out the ocean freight, the land freight to port, and the cost of the tractor itself.

But don't shoot the customer.

Believe me, we thought about firing him, this time!

Still, it was an opportunity for us to shore up our ocean freight solution. Things happen on the open water – but cargo offloading should be an extremely rare thing, and we should have a few more strings to pull when something comes up.

Not to mention that this type of customer should probably pay up front. Lesson learned!

The voicemail light is blinking again… caller ID says it's the freight forwarder. Not again…

Right, Mike?

Opportunity is missed by most people because it is dressed in overalls and looks like work.

Thomas Edison

The project team sat down together for their umpteenth meeting. This project hadn't been going very well. Engineering and pilot builds had taken two years, and the end did not appear to be in sight.

The team was gathered to try and sketch out a plan update that would identify how much delay (and, how much additional cost) would be required to bring the new design to launch.

The project manager called the meeting to order. "Well, we didn't get the testing done, we're over cost and over budget, and we still have a lot of new designs to finish, but what else is new?"

Already, your author's gut is going off. We're not really trying to be productive here, are we?

"So we need to put A, B, C in the spreadsheet here, and then work up a plan for D, and then you, you, and you need to get back to us on E, F, and G."

"Right, Mike?" Our PM beams a smile around the room as if to say, "I got that right, didn't I?"

The facial expression said it all. The biggest smiley face you have ever seen. Totally relaxed. And the eyes... clueless.

This PM didn't have any ownership of the project. He was only there to call the meetings, give the orders, drop in little bits of project management wisdom, and then complain if team members didn't comply.

Who was the manager with the clue?

Mike.

All too often, Mike would respond to our PM. "Well, Mr. PM, it's sort of like that. But we really need to think about H, I, and J which you didn't mention."

To which PM would reply, "That's right, Mike. H, I, and J. I was getting to that." No, you weren't.

If Mr. PM was new to the job, yes, of course. This would be par for the course. Experienced team members would groan and say, "Why'd we hire this guy?" Then they would move on to the work.

Don't Shoot the Customer!

But Mr. PM had been in the job nearly a year. And, though Mike knew how things should go, he hired Mr. PM to manage the project. If Mike was sprinkling advice to Mr. PM, and Mr. PM was sprinkling advice to the team members, who was managing the project?

Nobody.

After one or two more of these meetings, I'm sure appetites would be strongly in favor of shooting this customer!

As it turned out, the project continued to balloon over its budget until your author put together the spreadsheet that mattered. Mike's superiors stepped in to aggressively manage the project from that point forward.

What's a team member to do in this situation?

The gut instinct (and the typical approach) is to try to get the project manager removed. However, this is a high risk, low payoff scenario which often backfires and causes the team member to be removed, instead!

I agree, you don't really want to carry Mr. PM. Besides, project management might not be your strong suit. You'd be fooling yourself to think you can take over the job and work your own responsibilities as well.

However, Mr. PM isn't doing the job. Your salvation will be to develop a relationship with Mike to gain an appreciation for which way this project should be going. It wouldn't hurt to keep a communication channel open with your fellow team members, as well. Then, when Mr. PM gives his spiel, you will be smiling as you clarify one or two points that will REALLY help to keep the project moving!

Customer feedback at its finest

Nothing worth having comes easy.

Theodore Roosevelt

History (or, possibly, legend) places the invention of the Potato Chip in the hands of one George Crum sometime in the 1850's.

Crum, a resort chef in New York, was trying to satisfy a customer who thought the French fries were too thick. In the modern era where steak fries are in, this might be hard to imagine! Obligingly, he made a thinner batch, and then a thinner one, but this discriminating diner could not be satisfied.

"You shouldn't need a fork to eat these!"

Don't Shoot the Customer!

Out of sheer frustration, Crum cut the next fries down so thin that they resembled thin discs and fried 'em up. You definitely could not eat <u>these</u> with a fork! They didn't hold their shape very well, having been warped by the hot cooking oil. They were a bit crispier than fries, too. Sort of like a steak that's on the well side of well done.

"Your fries, sir."

The diner let them cool a bit and then picked one up. My, these were weird looking – could they be perhaps a little burnt? He ate one. And another. The diner was now… delighted!

And now, thanks to a few enterprising manufacturers and marketers, we can't get enough of these potato chips.

Do you know a good caterer?

I know right from wrong. WRONG is the fun one.

Pointless Poster on Pinterest

Our business was growing, and we had multiple vendors to perform all the services we needed in case one of our vendors had a conflict with an event of ours. I had a discussion with one of our caterers about why she was not being called by the brides we referred to her.

It was puzzling, her prices were spot on! Her quality of work was over the top and she was a great asset to us, but after I would sell the customer on her, the brides did not book an appointment to meet with her.

We both needed to discover what was going wrong.

A few weeks later, a bride-to-be was on tour at our wedding venue, seeing how her event would go and the resources she would need. The caterer was next on the list. We opened our design resource book and scanned the caterers. The bride to be asked to go to this caterer's page on Facebook.

"Whose page is that"?

Your author had pulled up the correct page, but it wasn't her logo or catering pictures, food photos or place settings that were coming up – it was the caterer's personal page, beach photos and all!

After the bride left, I contacted the caterer to let her know I understood why the brides were not calling her. Her Facebook page was more of a promotion of various travel destinations than her very fine cooking and catering skills. Now her Facebook is updated and all those couples in love out there are responding well with the likes and comments on her skills and she is a regular caterer for our business.

Don't Shoot the Customer!

The moral of the story: don't mix your business life with your personal life. Your customer wants to know they can trust you, work with you and that you will serve them for the best day of their life. They don't need to know where you vacation.

An In-Decision

It's time to come clean.

You know you've got one of those little storage units, right?

Where you've got the junk that you haven't looked at in years? Or maybe it's in your garage, if you like to leave your cars in the UV radiation and bake the paint.

Our couple for this story apparently had a garage-full already, and a storage unit at one of those places with the electronic gate and the guy or gal in the office who sort of looks like they live there! They paid on that thing for 6 years. Can you believe? Every so often the couple would fall behind on their payments and would fight about catching up.

"Myrtle, we don't need any of that #$%&! I'm going to get a dumpster over there right now."

"Oh, Earl. Don't you rush off to do that! I caught that bill up last week!"

On and on, it went.

Until the apocalypse happened – a flood that wiped out the whole area where that storage facility was sitting. The guy in the office (naturally) didn't show up for a while. Months passed. Earl must have figured that Myrtle snuck over there and caught up the bill again. Only this time, she didn't. Common sense, perhaps? The units were more like dumps than storage now.

A few more months went by. Earl got a letter in the mail that looked suspiciously like one of those bill-collector things.   (Yeah, don't act like you never got one before) Except this one was from the storage unit, claiming $1,900 in back rent?

Come on, now. That was either a palatial storage mansion or a very long time unpaid. But the owner really felt it about the flood and all. He said, we'll settle for $500.

Earl was mad! "I'll march down there and pay him $1 at a time til we reach $500! I'm paying for mold and rat dust, now! Why would the owner make me pay for that – even $500?"

I don't know where he was going to get so many $1 bills. But he was determined to make a statement.

"You kept your stuff in there, didn't you?" Your author reminded him.

Never mind the $9,000 our friends paid before the flood – which touched off a fresh wave of anger in Earl.

"You left your junk in there – your 'in-decision' cost you a ton of money. You ought to be thanking the storage guy for writing your junk down to $500!"

Earl didn't even need to clear the unit out. He happily paid the owner 5 crisp new $100's and went to watch the football game.

Now, let's talk about YOUR garage and storage unit…

Sometimes, we have bright ideas.

Our wedding venue business is a labor of LOVE! We have a beautiful venue that our customers LOVE! As a developing business, we occasionally make decisions we think will make our customers happy and our business stronger.

We work 'em up.
Build 'em out.
That's what we did.

We wrote a STUPENDOUS contract document for our wedding venue and services. This was a serious upgrade!

Tons of options clearly and vividly described.
More professional.
More sales for us!
More happy couples.
We printed it out.
Handed 'em out to new prospects and then we looked at the stats.

New bookings had dropped to ZERO! How could that be?

Good thing we had some weddings booked already, or we'd be in a sorry state indeed. We handed out more and more, we mailed them to folks who looked at us before but didn't commit to us. Same result, which was no result.

We felt frustrated and exasperated (instead of excited and inviting) when our next new prospect arrived for a tour. I showed her the exterior grounds, the beautiful gardens, the special photo nooks, and then we went inside to see the chapel, dining room, and the dressing rooms. After the tour I handed her my new and improved (but failing) contract package.

She looked over the three very fluffy contracts and then looked at me (in slow motion, it seemed) and said, "What is the difference between these contracts?"

I thought to myself, Difference? Where did that come from? Isn't she looking at the savings? I spent a long time pricing out those pricing sheets, formatting them with an elegant font, and choosing the paper to print them on and…

Bride: "I don't get it."

Me: "Get what?"

Bride: "What are you trying to sell me?"

Me: "We are showing you, completely and clearly, what you are getting, what the options are, how much they cost, why one option is better than another, how much money you'll save. This way you will know what's best for you because we spelled it all out in plain English!"

Bride: "But there are too many options! There are too, too many pages. What's the *difference* between them all?

Me: "Well, you can see right here on page one, and here on page two, and here on page three! Here's the price change, here's what…"

Bride: "Couldn't you simplify this? We have a lot of planning and budgeting to do. Maybe a chart?" Her eyes bored into my eyes, seeking a simpler answer.

Unbelievably, our prospective bride made a huge change in our business by suggesting a simpler one-page pricing chart with one number on it. We got the message. We rewrote the contract, highlighting the services and price differences on one page. We took out all the fluff so it was quick and easy to read, and our brides could figure it out in 10 seconds.

Guess what? Sales came back.

Sometimes, your BRIGHT IDEA, is not necessarily the customer's idea of what is best. Sometimes, the CUSTOMER's bright idea is the best thing for YOU!

Keep that in mind!

Artists: Learn the Business

It's fun to have fun but you have to know how.

Dr. Seuss

Once upon a time, there was a naïve photographer (we'll call him Jim), beginning a career in wedding photography. Jim charged very little to get his foot in the door, to have clients to work with and build a portfolio of his work. There were no contracts to bother with, no legal mumbo jumbo, and no real foundation to build his new business on. Jim wouldn't demand full payment until all the photos were delivered! Sounds silly, doesn't it? It wasn't so silly when he understood he wasn't being paid!

The first deal Jim landed was with an old classmate and his fiancée who were looking for a wedding photographer. They gave Jim a deposit, and Jim told them not to worry about the rest of the payment until the photos were delivered. When the prints were delivered, the newlyweds' money was tight, and Jim felt sympathy toward their situation. Since he knew the groom from back in the day, all would be well, right? WRONG! It took Jim 9 months to get paid in full! It was one thing after another – an emergency, bad month for his friend's business, "I can give you $100 today and the rest in two weeks", and then, oh sorry, another emergency.

This went on for 9 months! Jim had bills to pay in his new business, also. Thanks a bunch, friend! It didn't take too long after that wedding for Jim to realize he had to build a business plan, or he would be OUT OF BUSINESS. Next, he needed a consistent payment mechanism to protect his company's image and assets. Nowadays, it doesn't matter if your customer is your best friend, brother, a 2nd cousin twice removed, or a successful business executive, if there is a financial transaction, you'd best believe there's a contract, on the day of the booking, and the balance due BEFORE the big day. Details of everything about the date, the engagement photos, wedding day, without being so overwhelming it scares the client. It MUST be a plan both parties agree to, in writing!

Artists aren't typically known for their business prowess (hence the term, "starving artist"). Great photographers sometimes fail, and mediocre photographers can succeed – both outcomes are based upon their business skills. Take the business aspect as seriously as the technical skills of your field, and SMILE!

Not the "Indy 500" we had in mind.

Don't Shoot the Customer!

"Tommy Hilfiger"

Me, sarcastic? Never!

T-shirt quote,
Qurious Shop

I woke up with a burning question in my head, "How can I market my venue to the local community?" There were a lot of options in all different price ranges, but which one was right for my business? Your author grabs a T-Shirt to get ready to arrange her venue to prepare for the next event.

First stop was the convenience mart to grab a sparkling water. As this was a popular morning stop, a long line of customers were already waiting with their coffees, donuts, chips, and waters. She noticed the other customers in line were reading the T-shirt logos of everyone else in line. Their eyes would jump from shirt to shirt while they waited.

What makes everyone do that? Herd mentality? Simplicity? Why do people subconsciously have this desire to read logo T-Shirts? What is this cultural phenomenon?

It's natural human curiosity, I suppose. If the T-shirt has a message on it, well, we read it. We can't help it. Today, though, not someone, but EVERYONE seemed to be staring at my T-shirt and slowly pronouncing the words on it. Why? Was it that cool? It was a top of the line, high quality black T-shirt with expensive gold lettering and glittery background.

Your author finally made it to the cashier and then it came out. The cashier took one look and asked, "What does your shirt say?"
I looked down at my shirt; half the letters were missing! It was a T-shirt for another business that I was wearing as a work shirt. At least it wasn't MY business T-shirt!

Wait a minute. Then it dawned on me, this is how I will advertise locally!

When you are out and about, wear a blouse or shirt with your business logo! Clean shirt, easy to read with all the words spelled correctly. It's an excellent promotion. Works on your car too. The T-shirt and car decals provide a "top of the mind" awareness and memory of when they saw the logo the last time. People will associate YOUR colors, your logo, your personality at the top of their mind and remember who you are and what you do, and probably where you are located. This even works over a long period of time if you only wore the color of the shirt with the logo.

But please, do behave when you wear it. Remember, you are being seen by po- tential customers!

Why are we doing this?

The first and most important sign of a breakthrough from a customer is when they say THANK YOU; the next most important sign is when they say something that makes you angry. Your anger is the clue to you, that your customer just handed you the solution to your company's next great opportunity.

--Lorraine Guerra

Two people, brother and sister, walked into a car dealership, known as the best in town, having been nominated 1ˢᵗ place for several years.

"Our father, recently departed, asked that we make a visit here regarding his will."

The dealer read the will, then looked at them, confused. Brother and sister pointed outside to the car they had driven up from Florida, still running in the drop-off lane. Father had willed the car to the dealership as a token of his appreciation for taking such good care of him over the years. He could have given his kids the car and sent a letter of appreciation to the dealership?

But, no.

The dealership had helped him so many times, they had earned his loyalty. To the end. The kind of loyalty we would all dream of if our customers would provide it.

If we could possibly earn that kind of loyalty.

It starts with not shooting the customer when they try to <u>help you serve them better</u> – but rather, thanking them.

Derek has seen his fair share of customer mishandling through experience in Corporate America – there's something about being cooped up in offices that tends to disconnect qualified people from remembering what customers want – and listening to them when they want something that would actually help them get where they are trying to go. He's on a crusade to get solutions and results for customers everywhere.

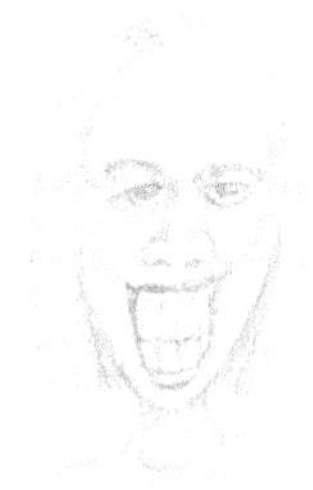

Lorraine has been an influential leader in many arenas. She's been directly involved with the customer experience, ranging from rigid government negotiations to corporate sales and small business. Her mantra: no matter how complex the interaction, all organizations have the same valuable resource: The Customer. In a recent interview, Lorraine commented: "The Customer is the oxygen that fills the company's lungs and brings life to any organization – they will also be that close friend that will identify missed opportunities, broken processes, a needed new product or service to enhance and expand your business, so long as you just listen."

The illustrious **Sarah** had a special heart for the customers who often don't have a voice – children! She started a nonprofit, "Will Paint for Babies" that raised money for Eastern European orphans that most people never even knew about.

Sarah's sketches add special color to our stories and help get our message across:
Don't shoot the customer.
Thank them.

Don't Shoot the Customer!

www.ingramcontent.com/pod-product-compliance
Lightning Source LLC
Chambersburg PA
CBHW050659250726
48662CB00002B/768